dabblelab

10-MINUTE
PAPER
PROJECTS

BY SARAH L. SCHUETTE

CAPSTONE PRESS
a capstone imprint

Dabble Lab is published by Capstone Press, an imprint of Capstone.
1710 Roe Crest Drive, North Mankato, Minnesota 56003
www.capstonepub.com

Editorial Credits

Editor: Shelly Lyons; Designer: Tracy McCabe;
Media Researcher: Tracy Cummins; Production Specialist: Katy LaVigne;
Project Production: Marcy Morin

Photo Credits

All photographs by Capstone: Karon Dubke

Design Elements

Shutterstock: AllNikArt, Aygun Ali, BewWanchai, Bjoern Wylezich, KannaA, StockSmartStart, Tukang Desain

Library of Congress Cataloging-in-Publication Data is available on the Library of Congress website.
ISBN 978-1-5435-9096-8 (library binding)
ISBN 978-1-5435-9102-6 (eBook PDF)

Summary: Need some quick and easy paper makerspace projects? They're all here! From flip-books and dream catchers to lanterns and locker magnets, these 10-minute paper projects will have kids making in no time!

All internet sites appearing in back matter were available and accurate when this book was sent to press.

Printed and bound in the USA.
PA99

TABLE OF CONTENTS

GOT 10 MINUTES?

Only minutes left of class? Grab some supplies and get making! These quick and easy paper projects are perfect. You'll be a folding phenom in no time!

Just be sure to leave enough time to clean up and put your supplies away when you're done.

General Supplies and Tools

paper
glue or tape
notebook
scissors
markers
pencil
paper clips
paper plates

Tips

- Before starting a project, gather the supplies and tools needed.

- Experiment and use your imagination.

- Ask an adult to help you with sharp tools.

- Change things up! Don't be afraid to make these projects your own.

FLIP-BOOK

What makes you smile? A funny-face flip-book
should do the trick. Improve your drawing skills
and have fun at the same time.

What You Need:

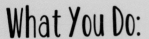

photographs of faces, all same size

notebook

glue

scissors

marker

What You Do:

1 Make sure all photos are facing up. Stack them on top of each other. Then cut the stack horizontally into three equal pieces.

2 Glue three strips to each notebook page. Cut the paper to match the strips.

3 Flip the strips back and forth to make mixed-up faces.

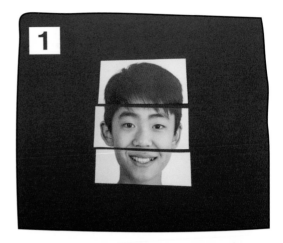

TIP Take pictures of your friends, family, pets, and even yourself to use in this project. Or cut pictures out of magazines or old books. Draw accessories, such as glasses, with markers.

NINJA CLIMBER

Only have one piece of paper? No problem!
With a few simple folds, you can make a ninja
that magically climbs up and down.

What You Need:

paper, 2½ x 11 inches
(6 x 28 centimeters)

marker

scissors

What You Do:

1. Fold the paper in half lengthwise. Then fold it in half widthwise to make a crease. Unfold.

2. Fold the right half of the piece downward to match up with the vertical center crease you made in step 1.

3. Repeat step 2 on the left side. Unfold both sides.

4. Using your right index finger, squash the right side of the piece along the crease. Repeat on the left side.

5. Flip the paper over. Draw a ninja face on the triangle tip. Cut off the tip.

6. Place your ninja between the two pieces of paper. Move one side of the climber up while you move the other side down.

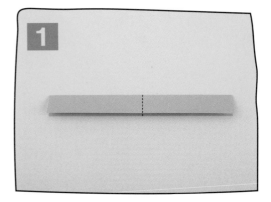

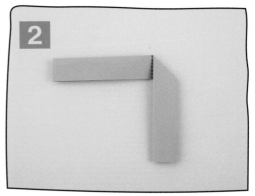

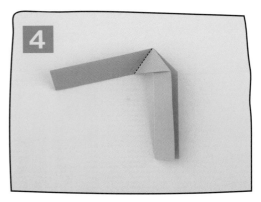

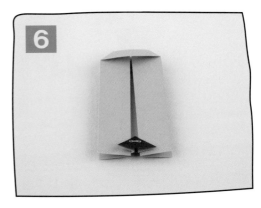

DREAM CATCHER

Roll up some old book or magazine pages
to make beads to hang from a simple paper plate.
Place this easy dream catcher in your room
to remind you to follow your dreams!

What You Need:

paper plates, different colors

pencil

scissors

yarn

tape

strips of paper (optional)

What You Do:

1 Draw a star or your favorite shape in the middle of a paper plate. Cut it out. Then poke holes with a pencil around the cutout.

2 Tape the end of a piece of yarn to make it pointy, like a needle. From the back of the plate, pull the "needle" and yarn through one hole, leaving a bit of yarn to tape to the back.

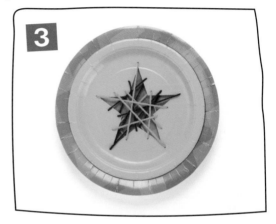

3 Then sew in and out of the holes. Tape the needle end to the back of the plate when finished. Tape a larger plate to the back of the first plate.

TIP If you have more time, roll paper with a pencil to make beads. String the beads onto yarn. Then tape the yarn pieces to the back of the plate so they hang from the bottom.

ROLL IT UP!

Got paper? Roll it up, and turn those
simple paper tubes into a stunning picture frame.
Just add your favorite photo!

What You Need:

scissors

old magazines, book pages, or patterned paper

glue

cardboard, cut to frame your picture

What You Do:

1. Cut strips of old magazines or scrap paper pages. You can make them any size you wish.

2. Roll the strips into tubes. Glue or tape the edges.

3. Put a favorite picture, or draw your own, in the middle of the frame.

4. Glue the tubes around the outside of the frame. Be careful not to glue them onto the picture.

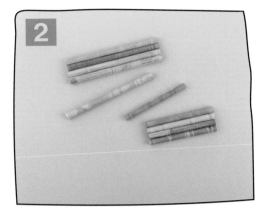

PAPER CHAIN BRACELET

Decorate your wrist with this easy paper chain bracelet. You don't even need tape or glue!

What You Need:

scissors

about 20 paper strips,
4¼ inches x ½ inch
(10.8 x 1.3 cm) each

ruler

What You Do:

1 Fold one strip of paper in half, then unfold it. Fold the right edge of the strip into the middle line. Then fold the left side to the middle.

2 Fold in the strip in half again. Set aside. Repeat steps 1 and 2 with the rest of the strips.

3 Slide the folded edges of one strip into the slits of another folded strip. Push it all the way through to fit snugly.

4 Continue adding more strips to create a zigzag pattern. Slide the two ends of the first and last strips of paper together to finish it.

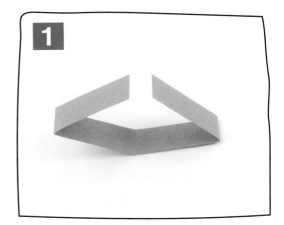

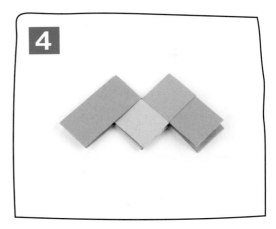

TIP Want to make a necklace or chain? Just make more strips of paper, fold them, and slide them on!

HANGING 3-D SCULPTURE

Take paper to a whole new dimension with an epic 3-D sculpture! Hang it in your locker or bedroom to add some fun flair.

What You Need:

scissors

card stock, different
   colors

What You Do:

1. Cut out a large shape from card stock. Start with a circle or square. This will be your center shape. Set aside.

2. Cut out several smaller versions of the same shape from card stock. Fold each shape in half.

3. In the center of the folded edge of each of the shapes, cut a slit. Make sure you don't cut all the way to the edges.

4. Open each shape. Using the cut slits, slide each shape, largest to smallest, onto the center shape.

5. Add more shapes to build a large 3-D shape.

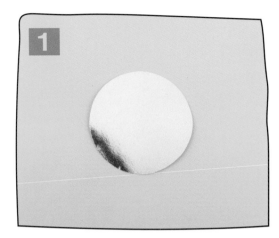

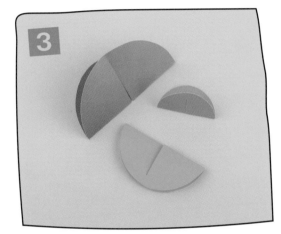

HIGH-FIVE
BOOKMARK

Need a hand keeping a page marked
in that book you're reading? Never fear!
The high-five bookmark is here!

What You Need:

pencil

paper

scissors

glue or tape

paper clip

What You Do:

1 Trace your own hand or draw a small hand on a piece of paper. Cut it out.

2 Cut thin strips of paper. Use a pencil tip to coil the strips.

3 Glue the coiled strips of paper to the hand.

4 Glue or tape a paper clip to the back of the hand to make a bookmark.

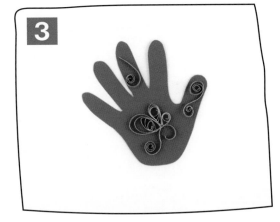

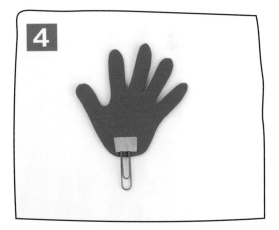

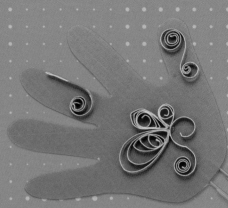

THUMBTACK
LANTERN

Light up your life with a colorful lantern.
On a cloudy day, it will bring the sunshine indoors!

What You Need:

pencil

colored paper or paper tube

thumbtack or pin

tape

battery-powered candle

What You Do:

1 Lightly draw a pattern on a piece of paper.

2 Use a thumbtack to poke holes around the lines of the design. Erase any visible pencil marks.

3 Roll the paper into a tube and tape it together.

4 Set the tube over a battery-powered candle to make a lantern.

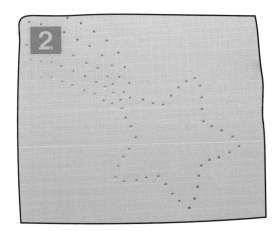

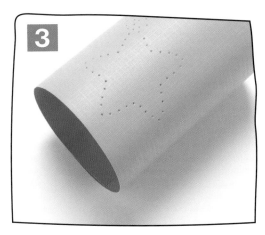

LAUNCH IT!

Draw or fold your own rocket and watch
it soar through the air. Launch away!

What You Need:

markers

card stock

scissors

paper clip

hole punch

hammer

scrap wood or wooden
   building block

2 nails

rubber band

What You Do:

1 Draw a rocket on card stock and cut it out. Decorate it with markers.

2 Unfold a paper clip to make an S. Bend one of the hooks to the side.

3 Use a hole punch to make two holes in the body of the rocket. Thread one loop of the paper clip through the holes.

4 Pound a nail near each end of a small wooden block. Stretch a rubber band around the nails.

5 Attach the other loop of the paper clip to the rubber band. Pull the rocket back and let go. Liftoff!

TIP If you don't have scrap wood, just flip a chair over, stretch a rubber band across two of the chair legs, and launch your rockets.

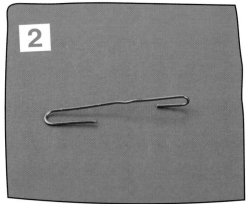

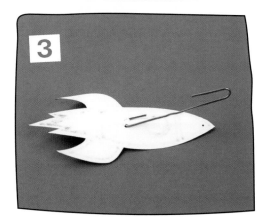

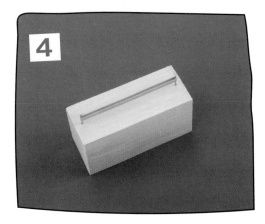

LOCKER MAGNET MESSAGES

You don't need a cell phone to send messages.
Surprise your friends with text message magnets!

What You Need:

scissors
dry-erase contact paper
paper and cardboard
glue
dry-erase markers
craft magnets

What You Do:

1 Cut text bubbles out of dry-erase contact paper.

2 Cut cell phone screen shapes out of paper and cardboard. Glue them together.

3 Stick the text message bubbles to the paper.

4 Glue magnets on the back.

5 Use dry-erase markers to write some fun messages to a friend.

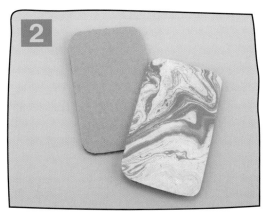

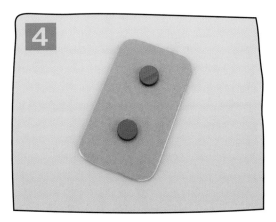

TIP Use a magnet to attach the dry-erase pen to your friend's locker. Your friend will be able to reply to you!

PAPER PET

What's your favorite pet? Don't have a pet?
Make your own paper pet to enjoy.

What You Need:

scissors

card stock or cardboard

markers

paper

What You Do:

1 Cut a pet shape out of card stock or cardboard.

2 Use markers to add some color to your pet.

3 Use paper and markers to make outfits, hats, scarves, sunglasses, or other accessories for your pet.

TIP Change the clothes on your pets to match what you are wearing. Or make uniforms for your favorite sports teams.

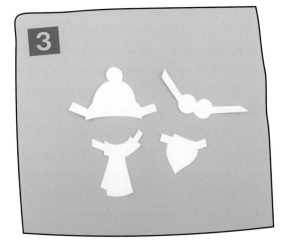

PAPER
SPINNER

Feeling fidgety? This simple paper spinner
should do the trick. Spin up some fun!

What You Need:

pencil
paper
markers
cardboard
scissors
glue stick
string

What You Do:

1 Draw two circles of the same size on paper. Use markers to color or draw patterns on the circles. Cut them out.

2 Set one of the paper circles on top of a piece of cardboard. Trace it, then cut out the cardboard circle.

3 Glue a paper circle on each side of the cardboard circle.

4 Poke two holes through the center of the circle with the pencil tip.

5 Cut a piece of string about 30 inches (76 cm) long. Thread the string through both holes, then tie the ends in a knot.

6 With a loop of string in each hand, wind the spinner, then pull. Watch it spin!

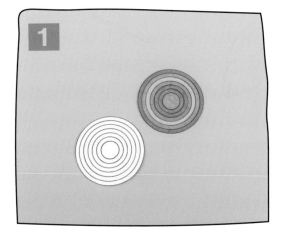

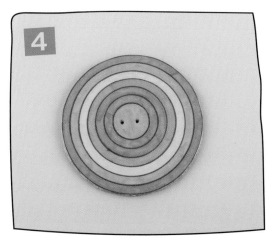

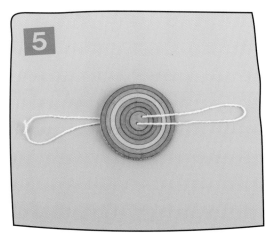

A FORTUNATE COOKIE

Show your friends that you care about them.
Fold these paper fortune cookies and write
encouraging notes inside.

What You Need:

- scissors
- paper
- glue or tape
- string and paper punch (optional)

What You Do:

1 Cut a circle out of paper about 4½ inches (11.4 cm) across.

2 From the paper scraps, cut a thin rectangle. Write a fortune on the strip.

3 Lay the fortune on top of the circle. Roll the circle into a tube and tape it shut.

4 Press down on the folded circle's center, then make a crease.

5 Pinch down the sides of the folded circle. Add glue or tape inside the crease.

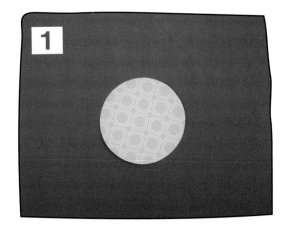

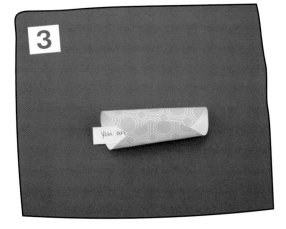

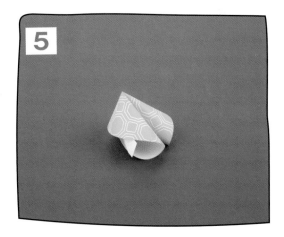

TIP String a bunch of fortune cookies together to make a garland or decoration for your room.

31

Read More

Buckingham, Marie. *Air Shark!: Novice-Level Paper Airplanes*. North Mankato, MN: Capstone, 2018.

Montroll, John. *Easy Origami Jungle Animals*. North Mankato, MN: Capstone, 2019.

Schwartz, Ella. *Make This! Building, Thinking, and Tinkering Projects for the Amazing Maker in You*. Washington, D.C.: National Geographic Kids, 2019.

Uliana, Kim. *Crafting Fun for Kids of All Ages*. New York: Sky Pony, 2017.

Internet Sites

Care.com:17 Easy Construction Paper Crafts That Any Kid Can Do
https://www.care.com/c/stories/3885/17-easy-construction-paper-crafts-that-any-ki/

The 36th Avenue: Kid Paper Crafts
https://www.the36thavenue.com/kid-paper-crafts/

Tinker Lab: How to Make Paper
https://tinkerlab.com/how-to-make-paper/

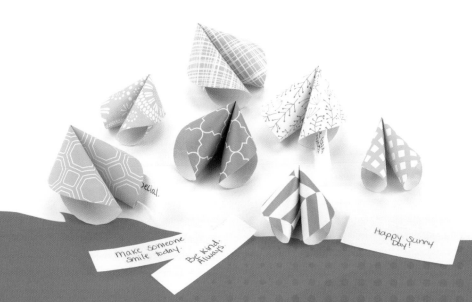